TRY NOT TO LAUGH CHALLENGE

KIDS VS ADULTS!
VALENTINE

Joke Book Edition
Valentine's Day Game Book

Howling
Moon Books

Try Not to Laugh Challenge
Kids vs Adults! Valentine's Day Edition!

Rules:

Pick your team, or go one on one.

Each team should face each other & make eye contact.

Take turns reading jokes to each other.

You can make silly faces, funny sound effects, goofy voices, wacky movements or anything laughable!

When your opponent laughs or cracks a smile, you get a point!

First team to win 3 points, or the most points, **Wins!**

Note:
You can make the game short with a total of 3 points, or longer with a total of 10 points, or more. You can split the book up and play in rounds, or go through the whole book until you reach the end if you want...it is up to you!

Why are astronomers hopeless romantics?

Because they always have STARS in their eyes!

What is a lovesick vampire's favorite song?

"Don't Go Staking My Heart!"

What does Cupid like to eat with his pizza?

Wings!

What indoor game is Cupid really good at?

Darts!

Why is Valentine's Day a volcano's favorite holiday?

Because it is a LAVA not a hater!

What was the most popular move
at the dentist's Valentine dance?

The floss!

Why didn't the girl want to go out
with the pastry chef?

She was afraid he would DESSERT
her!

What kind of egg is easy to love?

A HEART-boiled egg!

Why didn't the dogs stay
together very long?

It was only puppy love!

Why was the computer falling for
the WiFi?

He could feel a connection!

Why did the ghosts get married?

It was BOO love!

How do you spell hugs and kisses
in four letters?

XOXO!

What did the keyboard say to the computer?

You are just my TYPE!

Knock, knock.
Who's there?
Brie.
Brie who?

Brie mine!

What did the Star Wars fan say to his girlfriend?

YODA one for me!

How did the fisherman meet the mermaid?

They met online!

Why wasn't the couple in love?

They were only on cloud 8!

What kind card game do you play on Valentine's Day?

Hearts!

Why did the skunks get along so well?

Great minds STINK alike!

What did the little boat say to the big boat on Valentine's Day?

I love you a YACHT!

Why did the merman marry the girl-fish?

Because they were MERMAID for each other!

Why didn't anyone want to bring the math book to the Valentine's Day party?

It had too many problems!

What did the mozzarella say to his sweetheart?

You are GRATE!

Why did the computer fall in love with the keyboard?

It was love at first BYTE!

How does a snail sign its Valentine's Day cards?

SLUGS and kisses!

What did the monster say to his girlfriend on Valentine's Day?

I am heads OGRE heals for you!

Why did the cow kiss her crush?

She was in the MOO-D!

What did one canoe say to the other?

Are you interested in some ROW-mance?

What did the math teachers do at the Valentine's Day dance?

They exchanged numbers!

What did the crayon say to the paper?

I am DRAWN to you!

Where do computers keep their
Valentine's Day cards?

On their HEART-drives!

What triangle gets a lot of
Valentine cards?

Acute one!

Knock, knock.
Who's there?
Happy.
Happy who?

Happy Valentine's Day,
With all my heart,
I love you more,
Than a unicorn fart!

Who delivers Valentine cards to cats?

A litter carrier!

Why is love so strong?

Because love makes the world go around!

What did the caveman give his wife
for Valentine's Day?

UGHS and kisses!

Why is love blind?

Because you can't see it coming!

What do vampires do on a date?

They go out for a BITE to eat!

Why do dog trainers have
marriages that last?

Because they know how to STAY!

What is the poop emoji's favorite
song?

Love Stinks!

What happened after Cupid lost
his ID?

Now they call him Cup.

What did the painter say to his girlfriend?

I love you with all my ART!

Why shouldn't you bother sending a Valentine's Day card to a tennis player?

Because love means nothing to them!

What do you give a squirrel
on Valentine's Day?

Forget-me-NUTS!

Knock, knock.
Who's there?
Pizza.
Pizza who?

You have a Pizza my heart!

What did the piece of string say
to his girlfriend?

Will you be my Valen-TWINE?

How does an owl sign its Valentine cards?

OWL be yours!

Knock, knock.
Who's there?
Soy.
Soy who?

I am Soy into you!

How did the cellphone propose to his girlfriend?

He gave her a RING!

What is the most romantic city in England?

Loverpool!

What did the crystal say to his girlfriend on Valentine's Day?

Of QUARTZ I love you!

What vegetable gets the most Valentine cards?

The CUTE-cumber!

Why did the journal marry
the pen?

Because she finally found Mr. Write!

Why didn't the guitarist get a date
for Valentine's Day?

She was too picky!

Where do you go to find a good
Valentine movie?

The FLICK-ionary!

Why did the bald man marry his comb?

Because he knew he would never part with it!

What did Frankenstein give his sweetie on Valentine's Day?

A box of SHOCK-lates!

What kind of markers get the most dates?

The BOLD ones!

Why did the crab limp out of the
Valentine dance?

He pulled a MUSSEL!

Where does Cupid get his arrows?

Target!

What do you call two birds in love?

Tweet-hearts!

Did you hear about the two turtle doves who were going out?

They were very lovey-dovey!

Why did the puppet cry when he saw the Valentine movie?

Because it tugged at his heartstrings!

Why don't socks have long relationships?

Because they do not remain a PAIR for long!

Did you hear about the spiders who got married?

They met on the web!

What did T. Rex say to
the dinosaur?

Won't CHEW be my valentine?

Why did the man bring a rope to
the church on his wedding day?

Because he was ready to tie the
knot!

Why did the thread want to go
out with the needle?

He was SEW in love!

Why doesn't Yeti send out
Valentine's Day cards?

He is too COOL for that!

What is Cupid's favorite vegetable?

Artichoke hearts!

Why were the otters going out?

Because they were made for each OTTER!

What did the dough say to the rolling pin?

You got what I KNEAD!

What did the snowman say to his girlfriend?

I only have ICE for you!

Why did the girl wear a Valentine-themed sweater on February 14th?

She likes to wear her HEART on her sleeve!

Why didn't the dark clouds and thunder go out with each other very long?

Because it was a STORMY relationship!

What do you give a ghost on Valentine's Day?

A BOO-quet!

What did the farmer give his wife for Valentine's Day?

HOGS and kisses!

What did the porcupine ask his sweetie?

QUILL you be mine?

Why did the King of Hearts ask the Queen of Hearts to the Valentine's Day dance?

Because they were perfectly suited for each other!

What did the cat think about her
Valentine's Day box of chocolates?

She didn't care for the chocolates,
but thought the box was great!

What did the building block say
to his girlfriend?

I will never LEGO!

Who did the ghost bring to the Valentine's Day dance?

Anyone he could dig up!

Why do scientists question the phrase, "love is in the air"?

Because they can only find oxygen, nitrogen, and carbon dioxide!

What is a monster's favorite play?

Romeo and Ghouliet!

Why did the girl give the boy
a calendar?

He asked her for a date!

Why is February 14th a great day
for a party?

Because you can really party
HEARTY!

Knock, knock.
Who's there?
Purr.
Purr who?

You are my Purrfect for me!

Knock, knock.
Who's there?
Soda.
Soda who?

I think you're SODA cute!

Why did the two skydiving instructors go on a date?

They were falling for each other!

Why do ghouls and demons like each other?

Because demons are a ghoul's best friend!

What did the pickle say to his crush?

You are one in a DILLION!

Why couldn't the mummy go to the Valentine's Day party?

She was too wrapped up at work!

Why didn't the two rocks stay married?

They took each other for GRANITE!

What did the French chef give his girlfriend for Valentine's Day?

A hug and a quiche!

What did T. rex say to the other
T. rex?

You make my heart SAUR!

Why did the guy send his crush a
Valentine on Twitter?

She was his Tweety-pie!

What did the little mermaid say
to her date?

You are O-FISHALLY the best!

What did the marshmallow say
to the chocolate and the graham
cracker?

I wish I had S'MORE friends
like you!

How do you turn a raspberry into a
blueberry?

Don't ask her to be your Valentine!

Did you hear about the two cell phones that got married?

The ceremony was okay, but the reception was great!

What did the lake say to the dock?

You are PIERfect!

Knock, knock.
Who's there?
Bunny.
Bunny who?
No Bunny compares to you!

Why do skunks look forward to
Valentine's Day?

They are very SCENT-imental
animals!

What did the dog say to his girlfriend?

I Wuff you!

Why didn't the crustacean want to go to the Valentine's Day party?

He was too crabby!

What is so good about February 15th?

Valentine candy goes on sale!

Knock, knock.
Who's there?
Sherwood.
Sherwood who?

Sherwood like to be your Valentine!

What did the clam chowder say to the croutons?

We are SOUP-ER together!

Why were the turtles together?

They were TURTLEY into each other!

What vegetable is the coolest
Valentine of all?

The RAD-ish!

What did the gamer tell his
girlfriend on Valentine's Day?

Our love is on another LEVEL!

Why didn't anyone want to go out
with the shoe?

He was such a HEEL!

What did the mirror say to the artery?

You're so vein!

What did the heart sticker say to the paper?

I am STUCK on you!

What did the zombie say to her friends when the movie star asked her to the Valentine's Day dance?

Eat your hearts out!

What did the snail's Valentine's Day
card say?

Be my Valen-SLIME!

How do you get a muffin to go to
the Valentine's Dance with you?

Butter him up!

Why did the rock break up with his girlfriend?

He had a heart of stone!

What did the hook say to the fish?

You are a REEL catch!

What canary sends out the most Valentine cards on Twitter?

Tweety Bird!

Did you hear about the happy campers?

Their love was in tents!

Knock, knock.
Who's there?
Gracie.
Gracie who?

I am Gracie about you!

What do bats do on a date?

They HANG out with each other!

Knock, knock.
Who's there?
Jimmy.
Jimmy who?

Jimmy a kiss!

How does Santa sign his Valentine's Day card?

XHO XHO XHO!

How do you serve ice cream
at a Valentine's Day party?

You SCUPID it out!

Knock, knock.
Who's there?
Buoy.
Buoy who?

Buoy do I like you!

Why did the bug break up
with her boyfriend?

She was really TICKED off!

Why did the hammer leave the
Valentine's Day party?

He had a pounding headache!

Why don't digital clocks have long
relationships?

Their hours are numbered!

Why didn't anyone want to go
out with the cliff diver?

He was too jumpy!

Did you hear about cupid asking
the fairy out for a date?

He figured he would give it
a SHOT!

Why did the merman ask
the mermaid out?

Because he wanted to SEA her!

Why couldn't the artist buy a
Valentine's present for his sweetie?

He needed a job so he could
DRAW a salary!

What do you say when someone gives you a bouquet?

Thanks a BUNCH!

Why did the planet break up with his girlfriend?

He needed some space!

Why do tomatoes sleep in after going on a late night date?

Because they need to KETSUP on their sleep!

Why was it easy to ask a pastry chef for a date?

It is a piece of cake!

Knock, knock.
Who's there?
Tomatoes.
Tomatoes who?

I love you from my head Tomatoes!

What did the pie say to the cupcake?

I have a CRUST on you!

Why shouldn't you date a tree?

They LEAF every Spring!

What did the hog say to his sweetie?

Miss you PIG time!

What did the car say to the race car driver?

You DRIVE me crazy!

Kids vs Adults! Valentine's Day Edition

Thanks for Spreading the Love with these Cupid Approved Valentine Jokes!

Your smile muscles can now take a well deserved break after playing the Try Not to Laugh Challenge!

Please consider leaving us a review on Amazon.com. We value your feedback & greatly appreciate your time!

Howling Moon Books

Available from Howling Moon Books

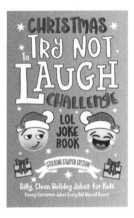

Available from Howling Moon Books

Available from Howling Moon Books

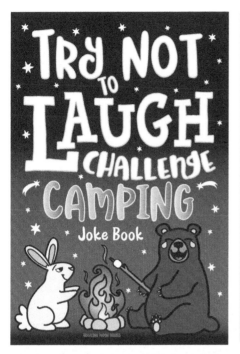

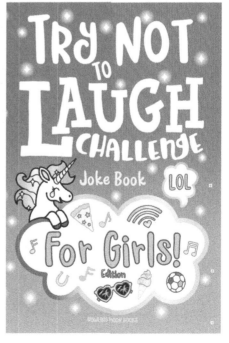

Available from Howling Moon Books

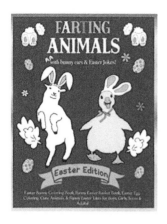

Made in the USA
Monee, IL
09 February 2023

27347142R00039